ENERGY-RESOURCE
MAPS

Jack and Meg Gillett

PowerKiDS
press™
New York

Published in 2013 by The Rosen Publishing Group, Inc.
29 East 21st Street, New York, NY 10010

Editor: Julia Adams
Designer: Rob Walster, Big Blu Design
Cover design: Wayland
Map art: Martin Sanders
Illustrations: Andy Stagg
Picture Research: Kathy Lockley/Julia Adams
Contributions by Richard and Louise Spilsbury

Picture Acknowledgments: All photography: Shutterstock, except: p. 8: Maher/Sygmal/Corbis; p. 9: Wikimedia Commons; p. 16: Joerg Boethling/Still Pictures; p. 26: Brazilphotos.com/ Alamy; p. 28: iStock

Library of Congress Cataloging-in-Publication Data

Gillett, Jack.
  Energy-resource maps / by Jack Gillett & Meg Gillett. — 1st ed.
     p. cm. — (Maps of the environmental world)
  Includes index.
  ISBN 978-1-4488-8614-2 (library binding) — ISBN 978-1-4488-8621-0 (pbk.) —
  ISBN 978-1-4488-8622-7 (6-pack)
  1. Power resources—Environmental aspects—Juvenile literature. 2. Power resources—Juvenile literature. 3. Power resources—Maps for children. I. Gillett, Meg. II. Title.
  TD195.E49G35 2013
  333.79—dc23
                                2012004334

Manufactured in the United States of America

CPSIA Compliance Information: Batch #B4S12PK: For Further Information contact Rosen Publishing, New York, New York at 1-800-237-9932

Contents

Introduction

This book looks at the energy generated around the world to warm houses, power transportation, and run factories. It looks at the location and distribution of the various energy resources that so many of us rely on.

The location of a country often determines what natural energy resources it has and how this affects its development. For example, countries with plenty of oil resources have grown rich selling oil to countries with little or no oil.

Globe shows the location of the map region

Fun research activity

Pictures highlight features discussed or located on the map

Europe: Fossil Fuels

Fossil fuels are coal, oil, and gas. They can all be burned to turn water into steam. The steam rotates the turbines and the generators that produce electricity in power plants.

Coal from the coalfields located in northern and western Europe powered the machines that started the Industrial Revolution in the eighteenth century. They made countries such as Britain, France, and Germany very rich. European countries that don't have fossil fuel resources or are running low on these resources import them from other countries or develop other technologies. For example, Portugal imports about 80 percent of its energy resources like oil and coal from other places. France produces 80 percent of its power from nuclear power stations.

Many countries in Europe are developing sustainable energy systems to reduce their reliance on imported fossil fuels and to be ready for the time when fossil fuels run out. For example, Norway gets almost all of its electricity from hydroelectric power (see p. 24) and Denmark produces 20 percent of its electricity by wind power (see p. 10).

The Ruhr Coalfield, in Germany, is one of the world's biggest industrial areas. Air pollution from its coal power plants has affected areas as far away as the Alps.

EXPLORE!
What does the divided bar graph tell you about Europe's changing energy supplies?

8

Today, fossil fuels are the main energy resources in the world. These are finite, which means they will run out one day. Burning them causes pollution and contributes to climate change, the biggest threat to our ecosystems at the present time. However, sustainable energy resources will become more popular in the supply of our energy demands in the future and they will cause less damage to the environment.

Each double page in this book introduces the location and distribution of energy resources in a different region of the world. A map locates relevant sites, and graphs and statistics provide important data. At the end of the book is a section you can use for further study and comparisons.

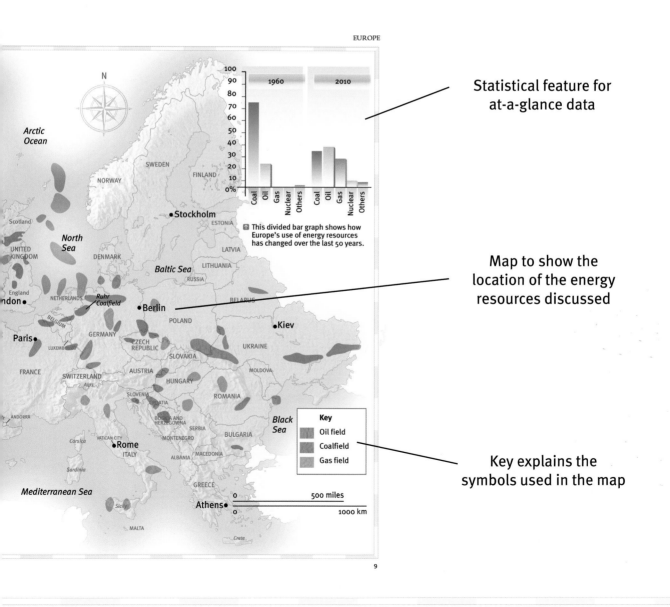

EUROPE

Statistical feature for at-a-glance data

This divided bar graph shows how Europe's use of energy resources has changed over the last 50 years.

Map to show the location of the energy resources discussed

Key explains the symbols used in the map

Key
Oil field
Coalfield
Gas field

The World: The Growing Demand for Energy

The amount of energy used by the world is constantly increasing. Our total demand for energy is expected to double over the next thirty years.

There are two reasons why the need for energy is increasing worldwide. One is that the world's population rises every year, so there are always more people needing to use energy.

The second reason is that more machines, from cell phones to cars, are being sold every year, and more energy is needed to make, distribute, and use them. This is why places like Europe and North America (see map and table) use more energy per person than a continent like Asia, even though many more people live in Asia.

The table and map also show that Asia is likely to have the biggest population increase and the fastest rise in people's energy needs, for example as more Asians buy cars. These ever-increasing demands for energy mean it is vital to find energy resources that are sustainable.

NORTH AMERICA

SOUTH AMERICA

⬆ The Tata Nano, made in India, first came onto the market in 2008. Its low price has made it affordable for many Indians to own a car. This change in lifestyle means that energy demands will rise in India as well.

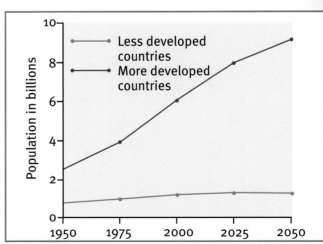

⬆ Every person uses energy, and this line graph shows how the world's population will increase.

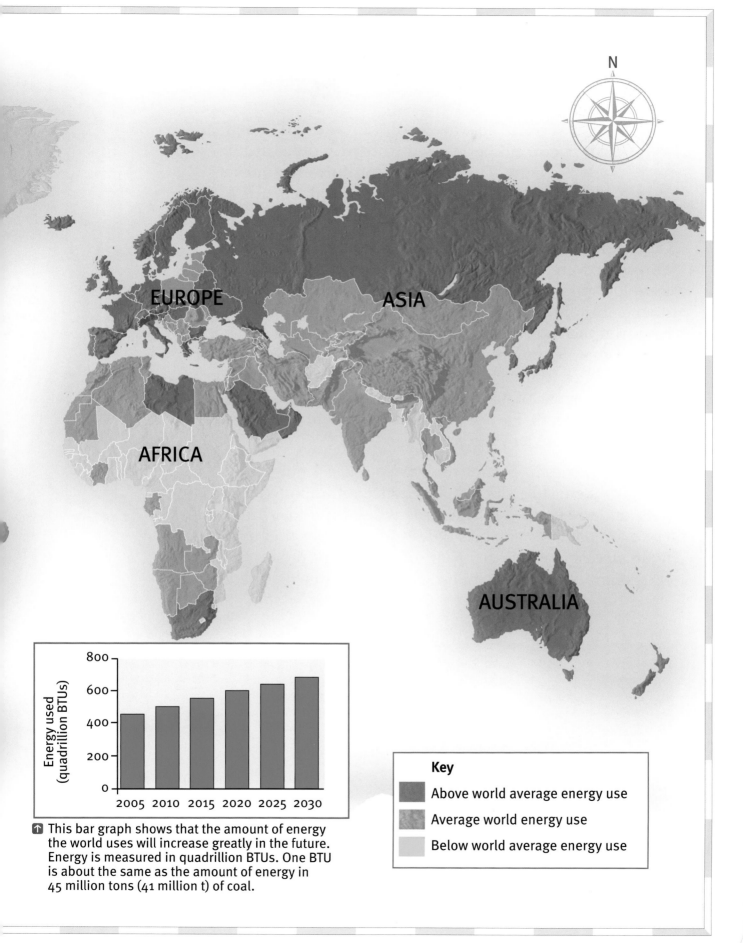

N

EUROPE

ASIA

AFRICA

AUSTRALIA

Key

Above world average energy use

Average world energy use

Below world average energy use

⬆ This bar graph shows that the amount of energy the world uses will increase greatly in the future. Energy is measured in quadrillion BTUs. One BTU is about the same as the amount of energy in 45 million tons (41 million t) of coal.

Europe: Fossil Fuels

Fossil fuels are coal, oil, and gas. They can all be burned to turn water into steam. The steam rotates the turbines and the generators that produce electricity in power plants.

Coal from the coalfields located in northern and western Europe powered the machines that started the Industrial Revolution in the eighteenth century. They made countries such as Britain, France, and Germany very rich. European countries that don't have fossil fuel resources or are running low on these resources import them from other countries or develop other technologies. For example, Portugal imports about 80 percent of its energy resources like oil and coal from other places. France produces 80 percent of its power from nuclear power stations.

Many countries in Europe are developing sustainable energy systems to reduce their reliance on imported fossil fuels and to be ready for the time when fossil fuels run out. For example, Norway gets almost all of its electricity from hydroelectric power (see p. 24) and Denmark produces 20 percent of its electricity by wind power (see p. 10).

North Atlantic Ocean

⬅ The Ruhr Coalfield, in Germany, is one of the world's biggest industrial areas. Air pollution from its coal power plants has affected areas as far away as the Alps.

PORTUGAL

Madri
SPAIN

EXPLORE!

What does the divided bar graph tell you about Europe's changing energy supplies?

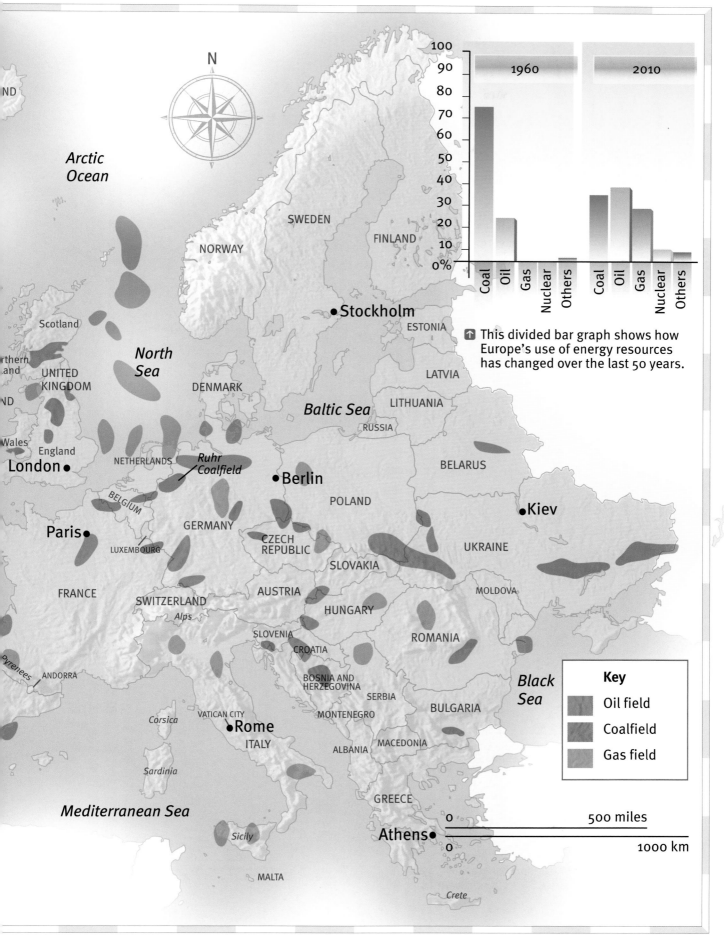

This divided bar graph shows how Europe's use of energy resources has changed over the last 50 years.

Key

Oil field

Coalfield

Gas field

Europe: Wave and Tidal Power

Wave and tidal power are both generated by the sea. Wave power uses the movement of the water surface. Tidal power is generated using the movement of water between high and low tides. Europe has a long coastline, which makes it ideal for generating both types of energy.

Europe leads the world in wave and tidal technology. The world's first tidal power station was built in France in 1966. The world's first wave power plant was built in 2008 at the Agucadoura Wave Park, in Portugal. New wave and tidal plants are planned for the future, for example a new tidal power station in Scotland in 2011.

These technologies do not provide Europe with all of its energy needs at present. Countries in Europe also use other forms of sustainable energy such as solar, wind, and hydroelectric power. Energy companies in Europe hope to share renewable electricity in a "supergrid" in the future. This would allow countries with wave power stations to import wind power from windier regions to fulfill their energy needs.

⬆ The world's first tidal power station was built across the La Rance river, in northern France.

ICELAND

N

North Atlantic Ocean

Scot

Northern Ireland

IRELAND

UNITED KINGDOM

Wales En

Londo

La Rance tidal power station

F

Agucadoura Wave Park

PORTUGAL

Pyrenees AN

•Madrid

SPAIN

0		500 miles
0		1000 km

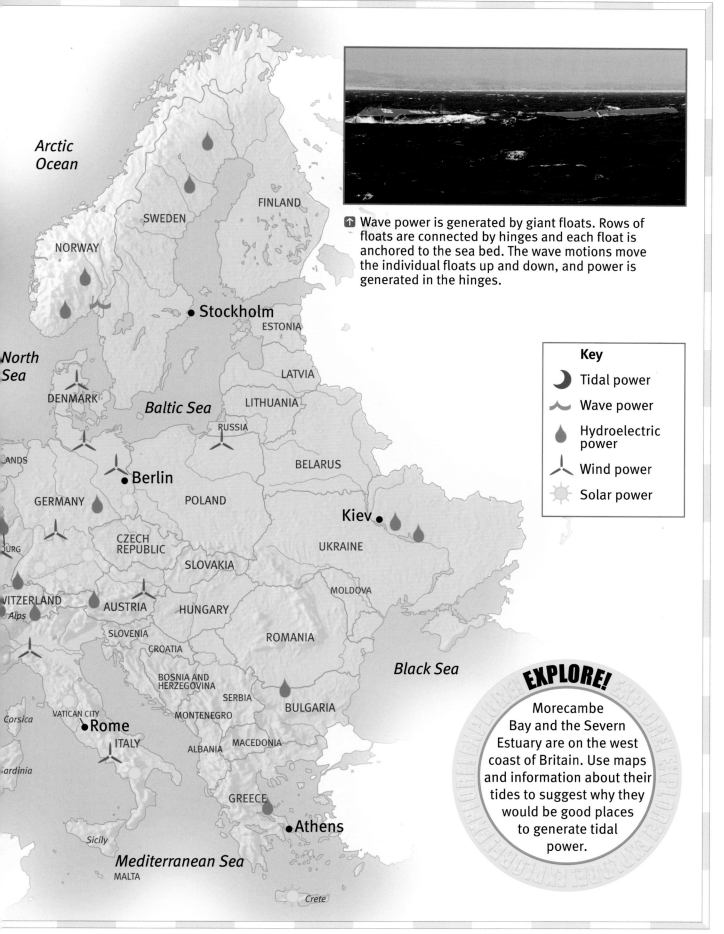

Arctic Ocean

FINLAND

SWEDEN

NORWAY

● Stockholm

ESTONIA

North Sea

LATVIA

DENMARK

Baltic Sea

LITHUANIA

RUSSIA

BELARUS

● Berlin

GERMANY

POLAND

Kiev ●

CZECH REPUBLIC

SLOVAKIA

UKRAINE

…URG

SWITZERLAND

Alps

AUSTRIA

HUNGARY

MOLDOVA

SLOVENIA

CROATIA

ROMANIA

Black Sea

BOSNIA AND HERZEGOVINA

SERBIA

VATICAN CITY

Corsica

MONTENEGRO

BULGARIA

● Rome

ITALY

MACEDONIA

ALBANIA

ardinia

GREECE

● Athens

Mediterranean Sea

Sicily

MALTA

Crete

⬆ Wave power is generated by giant floats. Rows of floats are connected by hinges and each float is anchored to the sea bed. The wave motions move the individual floats up and down, and power is generated in the hinges.

Key

🌙 Tidal power

〰 Wave power

💧 Hydroelectric power

Wind power

☀ Solar power

EXPLORE!

Morecambe Bay and the Severn Estuary are on the west coast of Britain. Use maps and information about their tides to suggest why they would be good places to generate tidal power.

Russia and Kazakhstan: Gas

Gas is the decayed remains of tiny sea creatures that lived over 200 million years ago and are now trapped in layers of porous rock.

Gas is a popular form of energy because it is easily ignited, giving instant heat. It also doesn't pollute the air as much as coal, and burning it doesn't produce any ash. However, gas is a fossil fuel, which means that it is finite and will eventually run out.

Russia and Kazakhstan are rich in energy resources, including oil and gas, which are sometimes found in the same regions. This is because both are trapped in porous rocks, which have millions of tiny holes (called pores) in them and occur in rock basins. These basins can be several hundred miles (km) wide.

Although this doesn't appear so on the map, Russia and Kazakhstan have over 30 percent of the world's total reserves of gas. Much of it is exported to the densely-populated countries of Western Europe. This is done using pipelines, which are a cheap and efficient way of transporting gases and liquids.

➡ This diagram shows a typical cross section through a basin of porous rocks containing oil and gas.

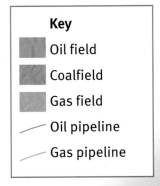

Key

▨ Oil field

▨ Coalfield

▨ Gas field

— Oil pipeline

— Gas pipeline

North Atlantic Ocean

An
O...

Nor
Sec

UNITED KINGDOM

IRELAND

London •

Paris

Loire

FRA

PORTUGAL   *Tagus*

Ebro

• **Madri**

SPAIN

EXPLORE!

Using the map, find out how many miles (km) gas from northern Russia has to travel to reach Ireland.

▨ Very hard rock

☐ Porous rock containing gas

▨ Porous rock containing oil

▨ Porous rock containing water

12

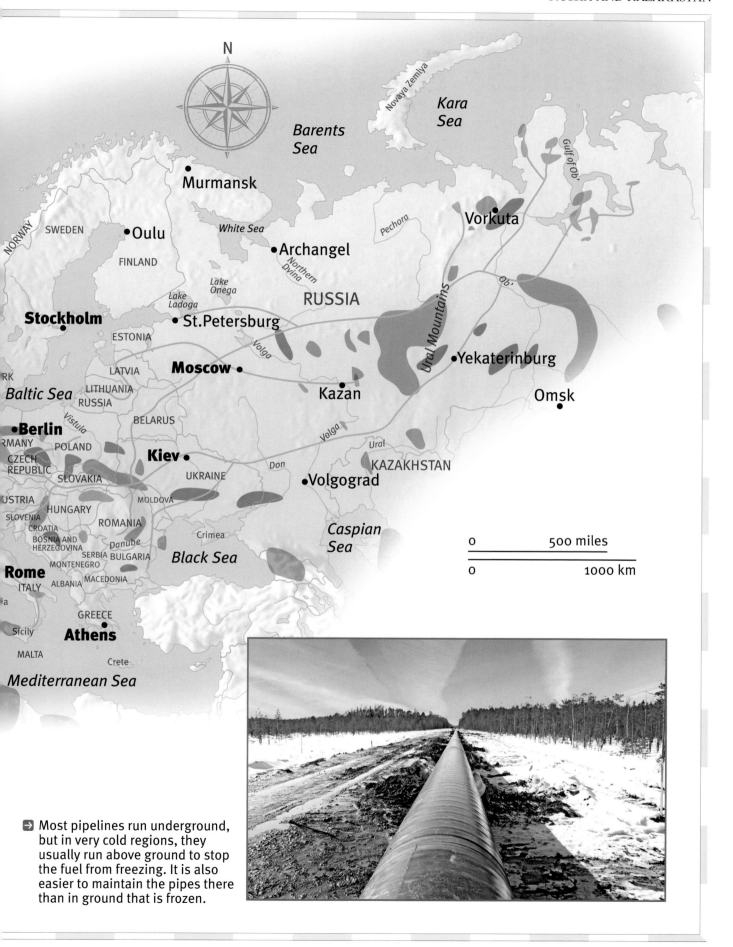

N

Barents Sea

Novaya Zemlya

Kara Sea

Gulf of Ob'

Murmansk

Vorkuta

NORWAY

SWEDEN

•Oulu

White Sea

•Archangel

Pechora

Ob'

FINLAND

Northern Dvina

Lake Onega

Lake Ladoga

RUSSIA

Stockholm

•St.Petersburg

Ural Mountains

ESTONIA

•Yekaterinburg

LATVIA

Moscow •

Volga

Baltic Sea

LITHUANIA

RUSSIA

Kazan

Omsk

•

•**Berlin**

BELARUS

RMANY

POLAND

Vistula

CZECH REPUBLIC

Kiev •

Volga

Ural

SLOVAKIA

UKRAINE

KAZAKHSTAN

USTRIA

Don

SLOVENIA

HUNGARY

MOLDOVA

•Volgograd

CROATIA

ROMANIA

Danube

Crimea

Caspian Sea

BOSNIA AND HERZEGOVINA

SERBIA BULGARIA

Black Sea

MONTENEGRO

Rome

ALBANIA

MACEDONIA

ITALY

GREECE

a

Athens

Sicily

Crete

MALTA

Mediterranean Sea

0	500 miles
0	1000 km

⮕ Most pipelines run underground, but in very cold regions, they usually run above ground to stop the fuel from freezing. It is also easier to maintain the pipes there than in ground that is frozen.

The Middle East: Oil

Oil has to be processed before it can be used. This takes place in refineries, which are usually on the coast. The oil is carried there in huge ships, called supertankers, or piped ashore.

Many of the world's largest oil reserves are found in extreme environments like deserts and stormy seas. Many of the Middle East's oilfields are in hot deserts or in the Persian Gulf. It is expensive to explore for oil and drill hundreds of deep wells in these places. However, oil is a valuable resource, especially now that other regions, such as Europe, are running out of it, so some Middle Eastern countries have become very rich by exporting it. Some are so rich that their people now have free telephone and medical services.

The economy of the Middle East relies heavily upon oil exports to North America, Asia, and Europe. For example, in Saudi Arabia three-quarters of government money comes from selling oil. Iran earns about 60 percent of its income from oil exports. However, like all fossil fuels, oil is a finite resource and may run out in the Middle East by 2090, so some countries are developing sustainable power sources. Iran is building wind farms and solar power plants to make use of the many hours of sunlight in the region and Abu Dhabi, in the United Arab Emirates, is building the largest single solar power plant in the world.

S
D

Sakākah

• Tabūk

Umm Lajj •

Me

Yanbu 'al Bahr •

Jedda •
Me

Red Se

EXPLORE!
Investigate what kinds of by-products are made from oil.

⬅ One of the many oil wells that make Saudi Arabia the world's biggest producer of oil.

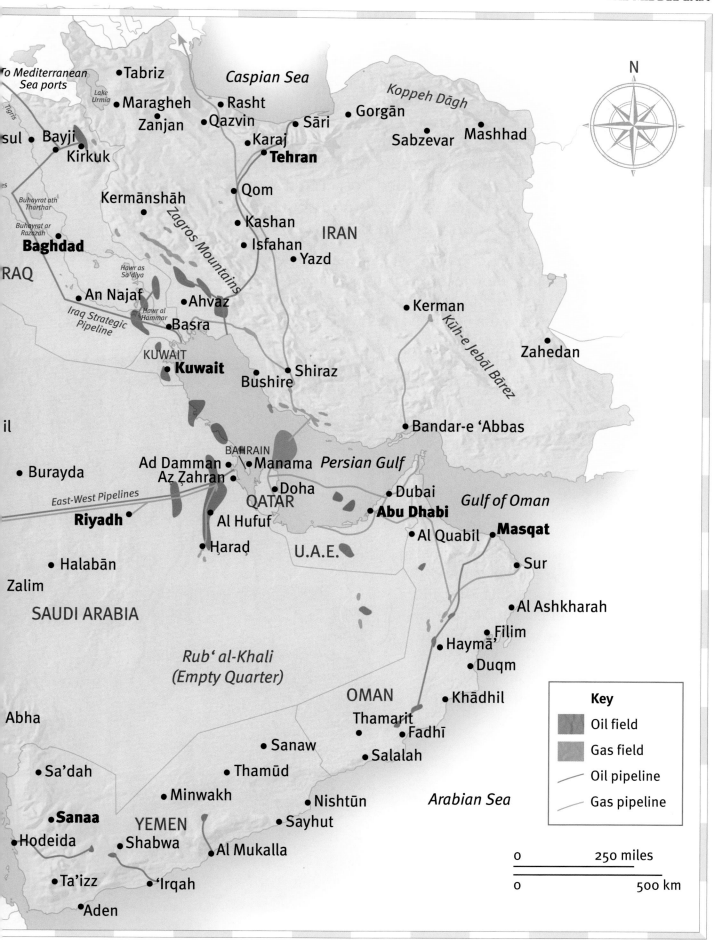

To Mediterranean
Sea ports

•Tabriz

Lake
Urmia

•Maragheh

Zanjan

•Rasht

•Qazvin

Karaj

Tehran

•Sāri

•Gorgān

Sabzevar

Caspian Sea

Koppeh Dāgh

•Mashhad

sul •Bayji

•Kirkuk

*Buhayrat ath
Tharthar*

*Buhayrat ar
Razazah*

Baghdad

RAQ

es

Zagros Mountains

Kermānshāh

•Qom

•Kashan

•Isfahan

•Yazd

IRAN

*Hawr as
Sa'dīya*

•An Najaf

*Iraq Strategic
Pipeline*

•Ahvaz

*Hawr al
Hammar*

Basra

•Kerman

Kūh-e Jebāl Bārez

•Zahedan

KUWAIT

Kuwait

•Bushire

•Shiraz

•Bandar-e 'Abbas

il

• Burayda

Ad Damman•

Az Ẓahrān•

BAHRAIN

•Manama

Persian Gulf

•Doha

QATAR

•Dubai

Abu Dhabi

Gulf of Oman

Masqat

Riyadh •

East-West Pipelines

Al Hufuf

•Al Quabil

•Sur

•Ḥaraḍ

U.A.E.

• Halabān

Zalim

SAUDI ARABIA

•Al Ashkharah

•Filim

Haymā'

•Duqm

*Rub' al-Khali
(Empty Quarter)*

OMAN

•Khādhil

Abha

Thamarit

•Fadhī

•Sanaw

•Salalah

•Sa'dah

•Thamūd

•Minwakh

•Nishtūn

•Sayhut

Arabian Sea

Sanaa

YEMEN

•Hodeida

•Shabwa

•Al Mukalla

•Ta'izz

•'Irqah

•Aden

Key	
▨	Oil field
▨	Gas field
╱	Oil pipeline
╱	Gas pipeline

0   250 miles

0   500 km

India: Biomass Energy

Biomass energy is mainly produced from fuelwood, crop leftovers, and cattle dung. Biomass plants use these materials to produce gas, which can then be used for heating and generating electricity for lighting homes and streets.

India is an ideal location for biomass energy plants because the country has many forests and many members of its population are subsistence farmers, so there are plentiful supplies of dung and crop leftovers. Biomass is also an ideal fuel because many Indian villages are in such remote locations that they cannot receive electricity from the main grid. The Biomass Energy for Rural India project was founded in 2001 to provide remote villages with biomass technology and teach them how to produce their own electricity sustainably.

Kasai was one of the first villages in India to have a biomass energy plant. It uses fuel from woodlands nearby, which is managed sustainably to ensure a constant supply of wood to make electricity. Villagers use this power supply for cooking, lighting, and heating. They are also buying more electrical machines like TVs, music systems, and computers, though, so the amount of energy they use has greatly increased.

The biomass plant in Kasai ➡ is maintained by one of the villagers, who has had training to do this work.

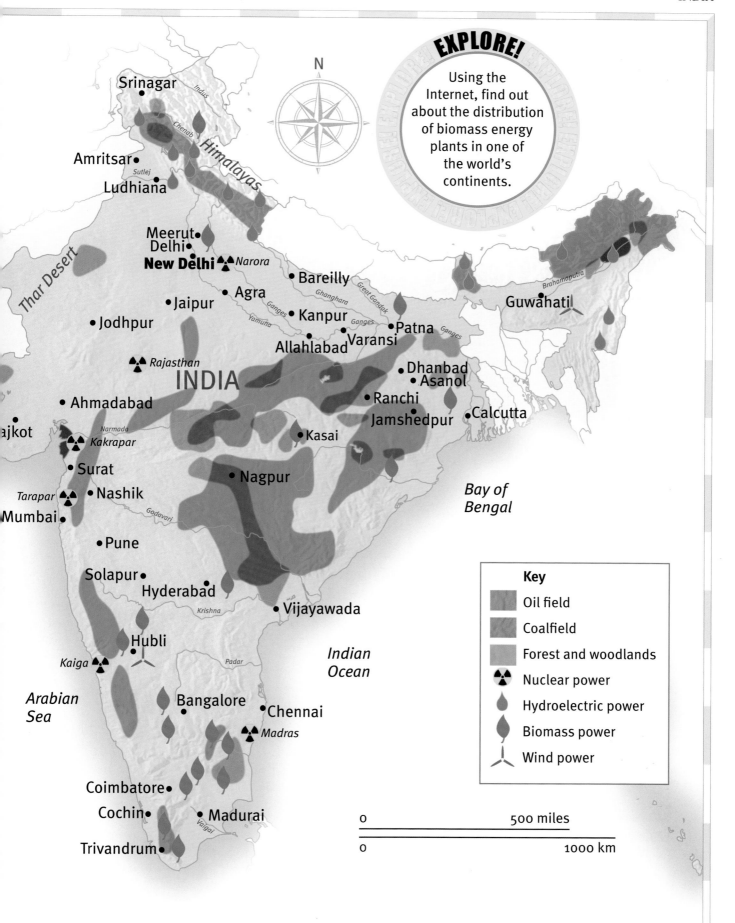

N

EXPLORE!

Using the Internet, find out about the distribution of biomass energy plants in one of the world's continents.

Srinagar

Indus

Chenab

Himalayas

Amritsar

Sutlej

Ludhiana

Meerut
Delhi

New Delhi *Narora*

Bareilly

Ganghara

Agra

Great Gandak

Jaipur

Ganges

Kanpur

Yamuna

Ganges

Patna

Ganges

Jodhpur

Allahlabad

Varansi

Guwahati

Brahamaputra

Thar Desert

Rajasthan

INDIA

Dhanbad

Asanol

Ahmadabad

Ranchi

Jamshedpur

Calcutta

ajkot

Narmada

Kakrapar

Kasai

Surat

Tarapar

Nagpur

Bay of Bengal

Nashik

Mumbai

Godavari

Pune

Solapur

Hyderabad

Krishna

Vijayawada

Hubli

Padar

Kaiga

Indian Ocean

Arabian Sea

Bangalore

Chennai

Madras

Coimbatore

Cochin

Madurai

Vaigai

Trivandrum

Key

	Oil field
	Coalfield
	Forest and woodlands
	Nuclear power
	Hydroelectric power
	Biomass power
	Wind power

0   500 miles

0   1000 km

China: Coal

Coal is the decayed remains of ancient forests, which have been compressed into solid rock over the last 350 million years. Coal has many uses, including generating electricity in power stations and melting iron ore in steelworks. It is also the raw material for many products that we use in everyday life.

China is the world's biggest producer and user of coal. China's coalfields are located in the east, so large amounts of coal have to be transported long distances to provide the rest of the country with energy. The location of the coalfields is also the reason that 60 percent of China's industries are in the east, including many of the steel factories that make China the biggest steel producing country in the world.

China's success in industry means more people can afford to buy more goods and this has increased the country's energy consumption. At present, coal provides about two-thirds of China's power, but it is also developing new hydroelectric plants, such as the Three Gorges Dam, which is the largest in the world.

⬆ Coal-fired power stations can cause serious air pollution, like here in Guangzhou City, China. The more modern power stations can filter out most of the smoke before it leaves the chimney.

KEY

▨ Oil field

▨ Coalfield

▨ Gas field

⬤ Hydroelectric power

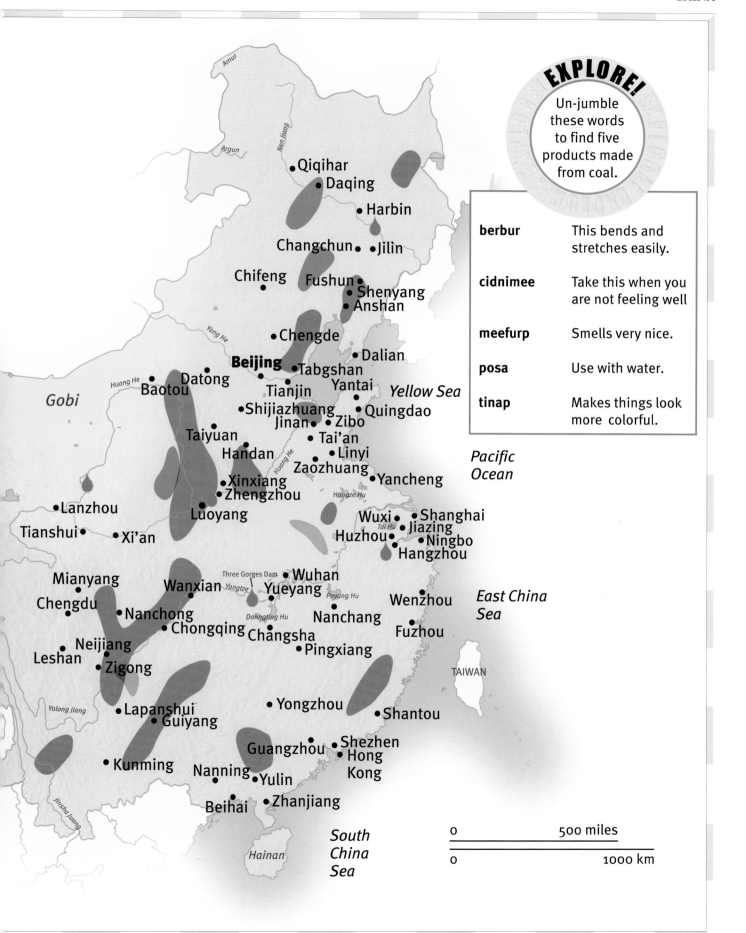

EXPLORE!

Un-jumble these words to find five products made from coal.

berbur	This bends and stretches easily.
cidnimee	Take this when you are not feeling well
meefurp	Smells very nice.
posa	Use with water.
tinap	Makes things look more colorful.

Gobi

Amur

Nen Jiang

Argun

Qiqihar
Daqing
Harbin
Changchun • Jilin
Chifeng
Fushun
Shenyang
Anshan
Chengde
Beijing
Dalian
Tabgshan
Datong
Baotou
Tianjin
Yantai
Shijiazhuang
Jinan • Zibo
Quingdao
Taiyuan
Handan
Tai'an
Linyi
Zaozhuang
Xinxiang
Yancheng
Zhengzhou
Lanzhou
Luoyang
Hongze Hu
Tianshui •
Xi'an
Wuxi • Shanghai
Tai Hu
Jiazing
Huzhou
Ningbo
Hangzhou
Mianyang
Three Gorges Dam
Wuhan
Wanxian
Yueyang
Chengdu
Yangtze
Poyang Hu
Wenzhou
Nanchong
Chongqing
Donngting Hu
Nanchang
Neijiang
Changsha
Fuzhou
Leshan
Zigong
Pingxiang
TAIWAN
Yalong Jiang
Lapanshui
Yongzhou
Guiyang
Shantou
Shezhen
Guangzhou
Hong
Kong
Kunming
Nanning
Yulin
Jinsha Juang
Beihai • Zhanjiang
Hainan

Huang He
Yang He
Huang He

Yellow Sea

Pacific
Ocean

East China
Sea

South
China
Sea

| 0 | 500 miles |
| 0 | 1000 km |

Japan: Nuclear Power

Nuclear energy is created when atoms of a nuclear fuel called uranium are split open to release lots of heat. The heat boils water and creates steam that powers turbines to make electricity. Most nuclear power stations are built by rivers or seas so they can use water from these sources to cool the steam.

Japan has few natural energy resources and has to import 80 percent of its fuel. In the past, it relied totally on fossil fuels, which it imported mainly from the Middle East. Today, though, 30 percent of its electricity is generated in nuclear power stations. Nuclear power is suitable for Japan because the country consists of four islands, so there is a large amount of coastline that has easy access to water for cooling steam.

Building on flat land along the coast keeps power stations away from the mountainous earthquake zones inland. If nuclear power stations are damaged, there is a danger that cancer-causing radiation will escape into the air. This happened in 2011 when Japan was hit by a tsumani, or large wave, caused by an earthquake under the ocean floor. The Fukushima nuclear power plant was badly damaged.

Japan is developing more sustainable and safer energy sources, such as hydroelectric and geothermal power plants. These tap into the underground hot water and steam created by volcanoes.

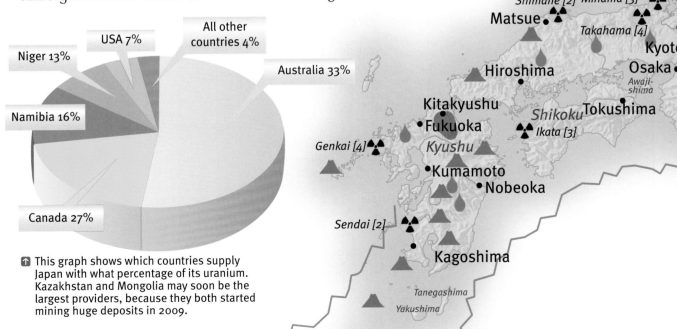

⬆ This graph shows which countries supply Japan with what percentage of its uranium. Kazakhstan and Mongolia may soon be the largest providers, because they both started mining huge deposits in 2009.

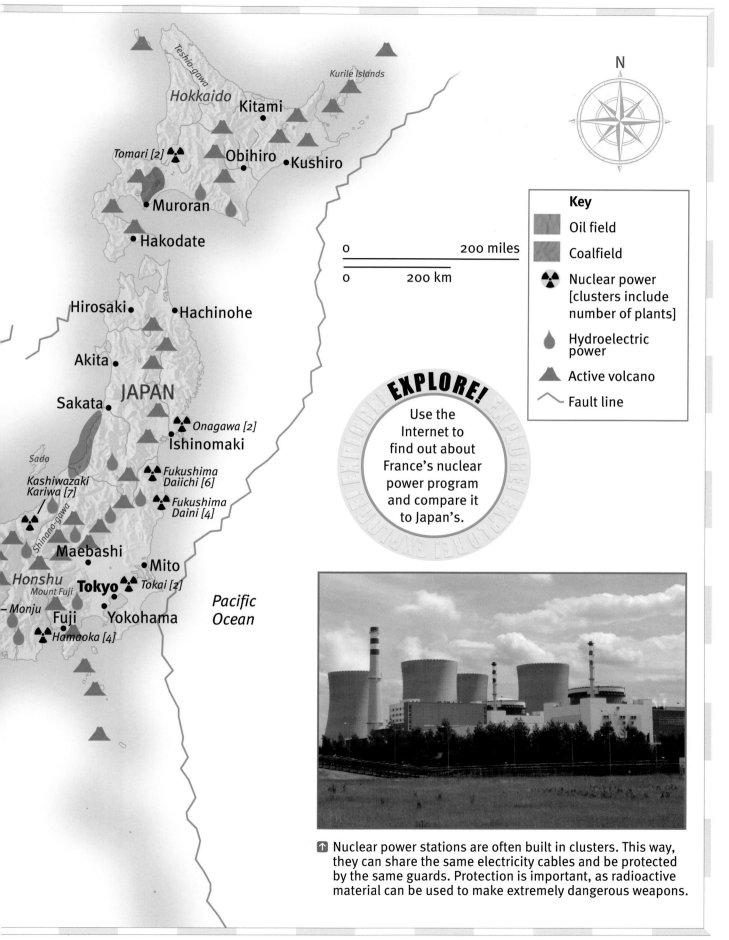

Teshio-gawa

Kurile Islands

Hokkaido

Kitami

Tomari [2] ☢

Obihiro

•Kushiro

•Muroran

•Hakodate

N

Key

▨ Oil field

▨ Coalfield

☢ Nuclear power
[clusters include
number of plants]

⬤ Hydroelectric
power

▲ Active volcano

⌇ Fault line

0   200 miles

0   200 km

Hirosaki•   •Hachinohe

Akita •

JAPAN

Sakata •

Onagawa [2] ☢

Ishinomaki

Sado

*Fukushima
Daiichi [6]* ☢

Kashiwazaki
Kariwa [7]

*Fukushima
Daini [4]* ☢

Shinano-gawa

Maebashi

•Mito

Honshu
Mount Fuji   **Tokyo**   *Tokai [2]* ☢

– *Monju*

Fuji   Yokohama

Hamaoka [4] ☢

*Pacific
Ocean*

EXPLORE!

Use the
Internet to
find out about
France's nuclear
power program
and compare it
to Japan's.

⬆ Nuclear power stations are often built in clusters. This way,
they can share the same electricity cables and be protected
by the same guards. Protection is important, as radioactive
material can be used to make extremely dangerous weapons.

Australia: Uranium Mining

One small piece of uranium can produce as much energy as millions of pounds (kg) of coal. Unfortunately, huge amounts of ore have to be mined to get even small amounts of uranium, so large areas of the natural landscape are devastated by the mining operations.

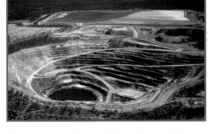

⬆ Olympic Dam Mine in south Australia is on the world's biggest deposit of uranium ore.

Australia has the largest uranium ore deposits in the world. These are located by the coast, so they can be easily exported by ship to other countries, including Japan. Australia supplies its own energy needs without nuclear power, so it doesn't have to process ore into highly radioactive fuel for power stations to use, or dispose of dangerous nuclear waste.

Key

	Oil field
	Coalfield
	Gas field
⬥	HEP
U	Uranium mine

• Darwin

U Ranger Mine

• Townsville

Tanami Desert • Mount Isa

Great Sandy Desert

Port Headland •

Ashburton River

• Alice Springs

AUSTRALIA

Gibson Desert

Little Sandy Desert

Warrego River

Barwon River

• Brisbane

Great Victoria Desert

U Olympic Dam Mine U Beverly Mine

Bogan River

Darling River

Lachlan River

Perth •

0   500 miles

0   1000 km

• Newcastle

• Sydney

• Adelaide

Canberra

Melbourne •

Australia uses mainly coal, oil, and gas energy sources. There are also hydroelectric power stations in the southeast, where there is abundant water. Australia has the potential to use more wind, solar, and tidal energy, but these are not being developed yet.

Tasmania

• Hobart

New Zealand:
Geothermal Energy

Geothermal energy uses natural heat from beneath the Earth's surface to make electricity. Most geothermal resources are in places where there are active volcanoes.

New Zealand is a good location for geothermal power stations because it has many hot, volcanic rocks and hot springs that can produce geothermal energy. Around 10 percent of New Zealand's total energy is geothermal and the rest comes from hydropower, coal, and gas stations. More geothermal plants and some solar and wind power are planned.

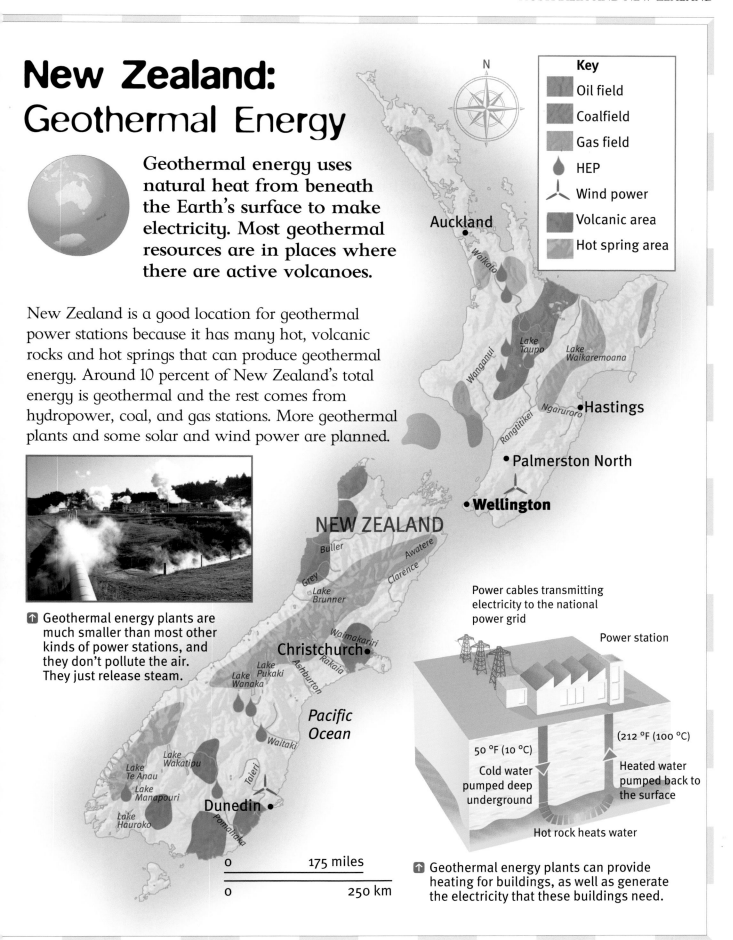

Key
- Oil field
- Coalfield
- Gas field
- HEP
- Wind power
- Volcanic area
- Hot spring area

⬆ Geothermal energy plants are much smaller than most other kinds of power stations, and they don't pollute the air. They just release steam.

Power cables transmitting electricity to the national power grid

Power station

50 °F (10 °C)
Cold water pumped deep underground

(212 °F (100 °C)
Heated water pumped back to the surface

Hot rock heats water

⬆ Geothermal energy plants can provide heating for buildings, as well as generate the electricity that these buildings need.

0   175 miles
0   250 km

North America:
Hydroelectric Power

Hydroelectric power (HEP) is generated by damming big rivers. The stored river water turns electricity generators built inside the dams.

Most HEP stations in the United States are on rivers in the mountainous western states. The Hoover Dam, built in 1936, was one of the first HEP stations. Today, it supplies electricity to 1.3 million people in cities including Las Vegas, Nevada. Canada is the world's largest HEP producer. Most of its HEP stations are along the Saint Lawrence Seaway in the east.

← The Hoover Dam created a new lake. It is called Lake Mead, after the engineer responsible for building the dam.

HEP supplies just 11 percent of electricity generated in the United States, but over 60 percent in Canada. The rest of North America's power comes mainly from fossil fuels and nuclear energy. Canada is also a major exporter of fossil fuel. HEP is not the region's only form of sustainable energy. Two out of three of North America's solar power plants are in sunny California and most of Canada's wind farms are near the windy Atlantic coast.

Arctic Ocean

Alaska (US)

•Anchorage

Yukon Territory

Rocky M

Britis Colum

Hawaii (US)

Honolulu

Pacific Ocean

Vancouver.

Washi

Seattle •

Orego

California

Sacramento

San Francisco

Las V

Hoover

Los Angeles

EXPLORE!

Find out about the negative impacts HEP stations have on the environment and in what ways they are environmentally friendly. Do you think that more countries should invest in HEP?

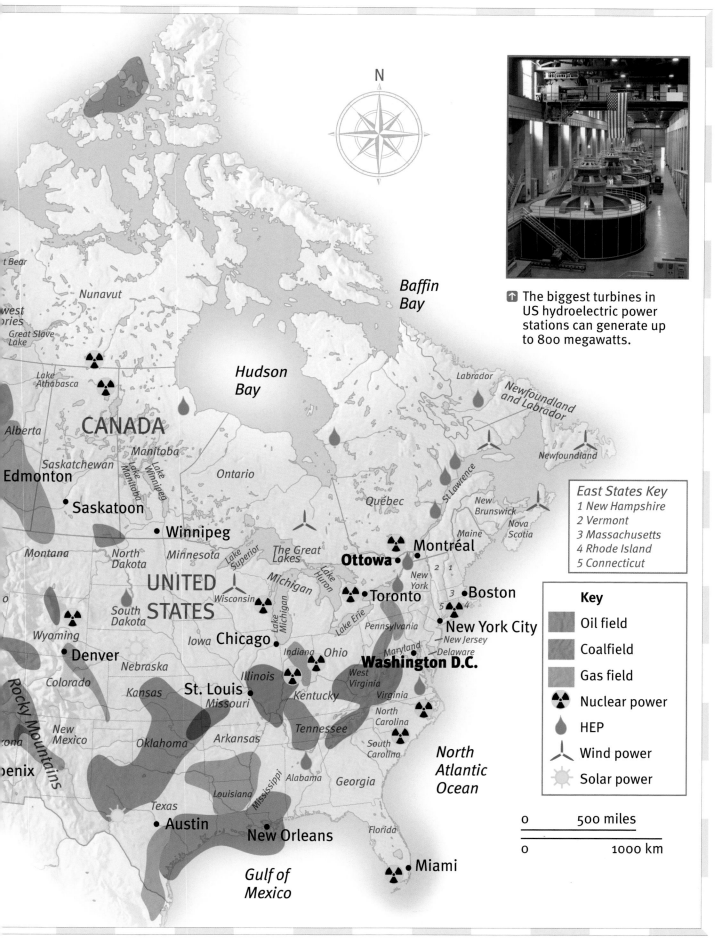

The biggest turbines in US hydroelectric power stations can generate up to 800 megawatts.

East States Key
1 New Hampshire
2 Vermont
3 Massachusetts
4 Rhode Island
5 Connecticut

Key

	Oil field
	Coalfield
	Gas field
☢	Nuclear power
💧	HEP
🌀	Wind power
☀	Solar power

0   500 miles

0   1000 km

Brazil: Ethanol Production

Ethanol is a colorless, alcohol liquid. It is produced mainly from sugar cane, a crop that grows best in very warm, wet places. This is why central and southeastern Brazil are the main sugar cane growing areas in South America.

Ninety percent of Brazil's electricity supply comes from hydroelectric power and the rest from fossil fuels. Oil for transportation, however, used to have to be imported from the Middle East. Then, in the early 1970s, the price of oil from the Middle East rose suddenly. This encouraged scientists to invent ethanol, a cheaper, alternative fuel. By making use of its climate and land to grow sugar cane on huge plantations, Brazil became the second largest producer of ethanol in the world and no longer has to import fuel.

To make ethanol, sugar cane is pressed to extract sugary syrup. Then yeast is added to the syrup to convert the sugar into ethanol. By 2010 Brazil had more than 10 million ethanol-powered vehicles. Also, nothing of the sugar cane plant is wasted, because after processing, its residue generates the heat and electricity needed to produce the ethanol.

Rio Negro

Rio Japurá

Amazon

Rio Juruá

Rio Pu

Amazon Basin

Rio Branco •

Chapa
Pare

← The ethanol is stored in huge storage tanks before it gets distributed and exported. This is an ethanol plant in Pradópolis, Brazil.

EXPLORE!

Investigate one negative impact that sugar cane plantations can have on the environment.

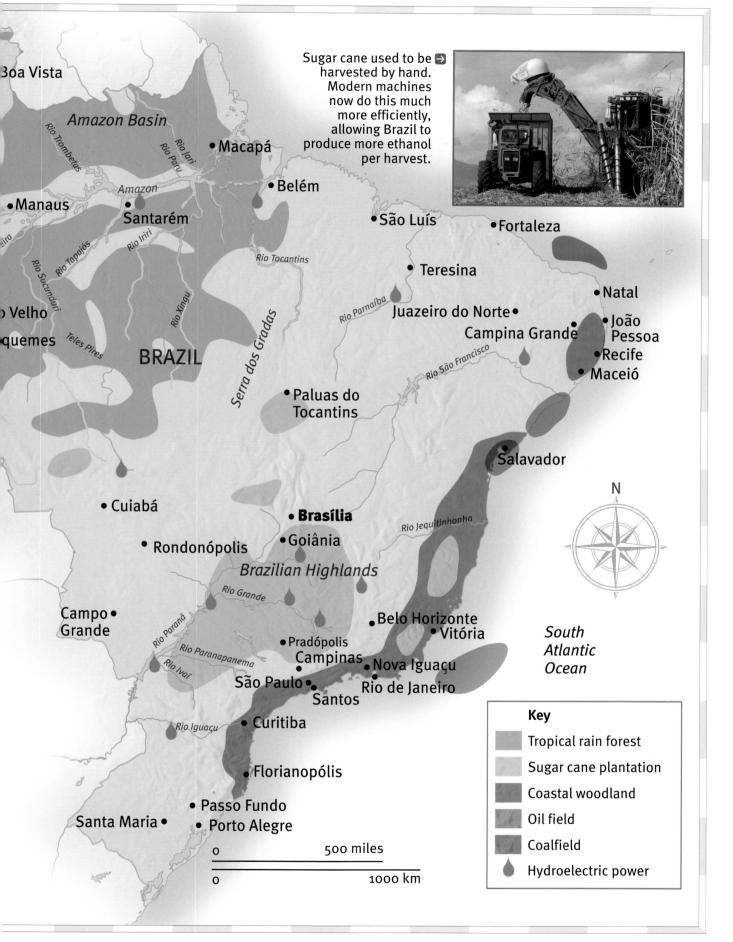

Sugar cane used to be harvested by hand. Modern machines now do this much more efficiently, allowing Brazil to produce more ethanol per harvest.

Key
- Tropical rain forest
- Sugar cane plantation
- Coastal woodland
- Oil field
- Coalfield
- Hydroelectric power

0 500 miles
0 1000 km

27

Africa: Fuelwood

In African cities, most electricity comes from coal and some from HEP. However, more than half of all Africans live in the countryside, a long way from electricity supplies. Most people living in villages can only get heat for cooking and washing by gathering wood for fuel.

The map shows the areas where people have cut down so much fuelwood that the environment is being damaged by desertification. This is when land turns to desert because all the trees and plants that stopped soil in an area from being worn away have been cut down. However, there are solar projects that could help villages that rely on fuelwoodto get their energy sustainably.

⬆ Fuelwood is the main source of energy for cooking, washing, and heating for most people living in African villages.

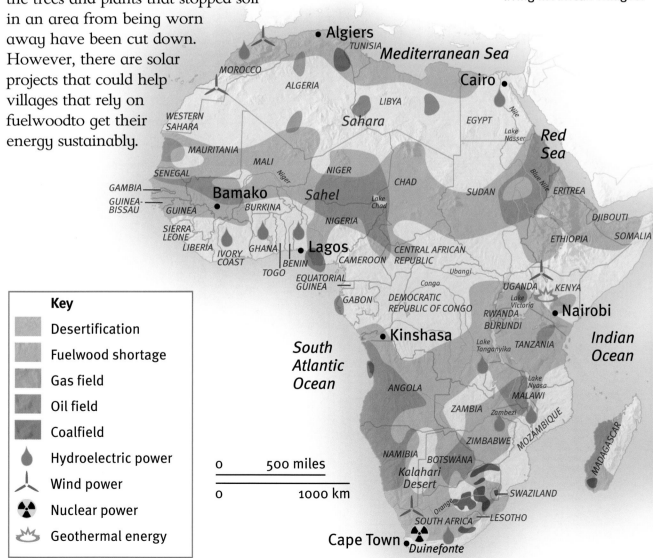

Key

- Desertification
- Fuelwood shortage
- Gas field
- Oil field
- Coalfield
- Hydroelectric power
- Wind power
- Nuclear power
- Geothermal energy

Africa: Solar Power

Solar power is obtained from the Sun's rays. The solar energy that falls on the Earth every year is over one thousand times the amount of energy used annually by every human being.

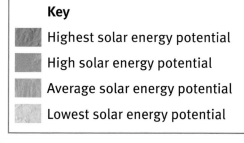

Key

■ Highest solar energy potential

■ High solar energy potential

■ Average solar energy potential

■ Lowest solar energy potential

Generating solar power is one way of meeting Africa's growing energy needs. The generating equipment doesn't have any moving parts that could wear out quickly, and it doesn't use any fuel. Solar power is very environmentally friendly.

The map shows the parts of Africa that are ideal for generating solar power. It also shows which countries are either planning or have already installed solar power stations. Generating solar power is one way of meeting Africa's growing energy needs.

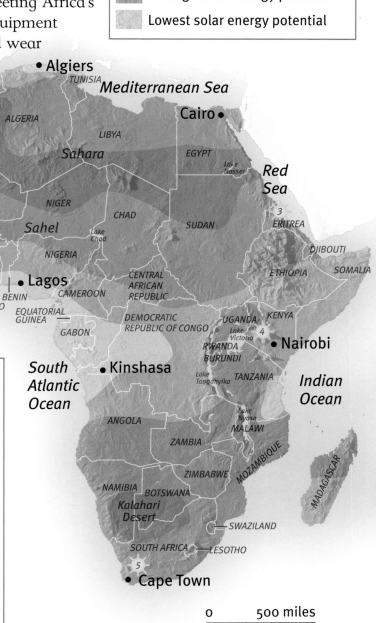

African Solar Projects

1. Morocco is planning to build a water desalination plant, which will use solar power to change seawater into freshwater.

2. Senegal supplies 10,000 homes in a remote coastal region with electricity generated from solar energy.

3. Eritrea has installed solar-powered water pumps to supply a number of villages with underground water.

4. Kenya uses solar power to provide electricity and heating for hospitals, schools, and village health centers.

5. South Africa has completed a solar-powered water heating system which provides hot water to the 200 houses of a remote village.

Now Test Yourself!

These questions will help you to revisit some of the information in this book. To answer the questions, you will need to use the table of contents at the beginning of the book and the index on p. 32, as well as the relevant pages on each topic.

1. Use the table of contents to find which pages show a map of:
(a) Russia's gas reserves.
(b) Japan's nuclear power stations.
(c) Australia's uranium mines.

2. Use the index on p. 32 to find the answers to the following questions:
(a) What is the location of France's first tidal power station?
(b) Who is the world's largest producer and user of coal?
(c) Which crop produces most of Brazil's ethanol fuel?

3. Use the glossary to complete a copy of this table:

Key word	Meaning of this word
Generate	
	Fuel for nuclear power stations
Mining	
	A group of wind turbines

4. Use p. 6 to explain how the Tata Nano car could change Asia's need for fuel energy.

5. Use p. 8 to list the three types of fossil fuels and find out why they are all finite resources.

6. Use p. 10 to explain how wave power is different from tidal power.

7. How does Australia meet some of Japan's fuel energy needs? The information on p. 22 will help you answer this question.

8. Which kinds of power station are shown in photographs A–C?

A   B   C

9. Use different pages in the book to explain how rocks and what happens under the Earth's surface can affect:
(a) where there are oilfields and gas fields.
(b) where it is safe to build nuclear power stations.
(c) where people could use geothermal energy.

10. What are the advantages (good things) and disadvantages (problems) about each of these sources of energy:
(a) coal?
(b) geothermal energy?
(c) nuclear power?
(d) ethanol?

Glossary

biomass (BY-oh-mas) Energy produced from burning plants and animal waste.

climate change (KLY-mut CHAYNJ) Changes in the world's weather patterns caused by human activity.

desertification (dih-zer-tih-fih-KAY-shun) The word used to describe the spread of the world's deserts.

energy (EH-ner-jee) Power produced by burning natural resources such as coal and using renewable alternatives such as wind power.

ethanol (EH-thuh-nol) A type of fuel produced from plant material such as sugar cane.

field (FEELD) A large area where there are important energy resources, such as a coalfield.

finite resources (FY-nyt REE-sors-ez) Resources which will run out at some time in the future.

fossil fuels (FO-sul FYOOLZ) Sources of energy (like coal, oil and gas) formed from plants and animals which died millions of years ago.

generate (JEH-neh-rayt) To produce electricity.

geothermal energy (JEE-oh-ther-mul EH-ner-jee) A type of energy produced by heat from underground volcanic activity.

hydroelectric power (hy-droh-ih-LEK-trik POW-ur) Electricity generated by river or reservoir water flowing through turbines.

mining (MY-ning) Digging materials such as coal and uranium from out of the ground.

resources (REE-sors-ez) Materials such as rocks, soil and water used to meet people's needs.

pipeline (PYP-lyn) A pipe used to transport large amounts of oil or gas.

pollution (puh-LOO-shun) Damage caused to the natural environment by people's activities.

solar energy (SOH-ler EH-nur-jee) Electricity generated using the Sun's rays.

sustainable resources (suh-STAY-nuh-bel REE-sors-ez) Resources which need not run out in the future if they are used wisely.

tidal power (TY-dul POW-ur) Electricity generated using the sea's high and low tides.

uranium (yoo-RAY-nee-um) A metal used as the fuel for nuclear power stations.

wave power (WAYV POW-ur) Electricity generated from the movement of waves on the surface of the sea.

wind farm (WIND FAHRM) A group of wind turbines which can generate electricity.

Index

Websites

Due to the changing nature of Internet links, PowerKids Press has developed an online list of websites related to the subject of this book. This site is updated regularly. Please use this link to access the list:

www.powerkidslinks.com/mew/ener/